WE ARE A REFLECTION OF UNITY

IRENE BOOKER

WE ARE A REFLECTION OF UNITY

IRENE BOOKER

This book is a work of fiction. Names, characters, places, and incidents are either the product of the author's imagination or are used fictitiously, and any resemblance to actual persons, living or dead, events, or locales is entirely coincidental.

ISBN 978-0-9906346-9-0

Copyright © 2014 by Irene Booker

All Rights Reserved

Booker Publishing
New York, NY 10022

Printed in the United States of America

April 2015

To order additional copies of this book, contact:
Booker Publishing
1-646-448-4781
www.irenebooker.com

CHILDREN RESPECT THEIR UNIQUENESS
BEGINNING WITH THE WORDS "I AM."

I am Change.

Page 5

I am Hope.

I am Gifted.

I am Love.

I am Thankful.

I am Peace.

Page 10

I am Dreamer.

Page 11

I am Unique.

I am Excellence.

I am Intelligence.

I am Courage.

Page 17

I am Humble.

Page 18

I am Patience.

Page 19

I am Grateful.

Page 20

I sfl1 Success.

Psge 21

We are the Future.

Together, we represent Unity.

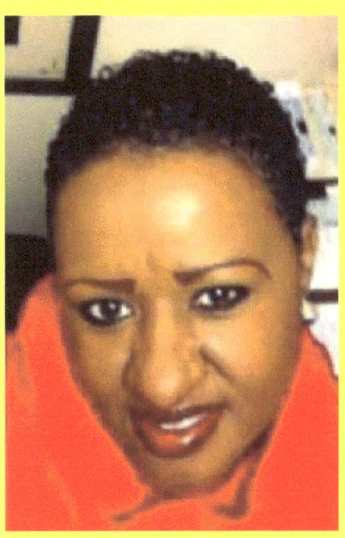

Irene Booker is a real estate professional and the author of Feelings From Deep Within, Prey of Innocence, The Seed of a Slave, Don't Be Ashamed Gabby, I'm Not, Dinner Table Conversations, The Legend of Mr. Have and Mr. Have Not, We Were Born For Greatness, A Young Mind, Knowledge and His Best Friend Wisdom.

www.ingramcontent.com/pod-product-compliance
Lightning Source LLC
Chambersburg PA
CBHW041542040426
42446CB00002B/202